Military Attack Aircraft

by Grace Hansen

Abdo

MILITARY AIRCRAFT & VEHICLES

Kids

abdopublishing.com

Published by Abdo Kids, a division of ABDO, PO Box 398166, Minneapolis, Minnesota 55439.

Copyright © 2017 by Abdo Consulting Group, Inc. International copyrights reserved in all countries.
No part of this book may be reproduced in any form without written permission from the publisher.

Printed in the United States of America, North Mankato, Minnesota.

102016

012017

 THIS BOOK CONTAINS
RECYCLED MATERIALS

Photo Credits: af.mil, Images of Freedom, iStock, marines.mil, Shutterstock

Production Contributors: Teddy Borth, Jennie Forsberg, Grace Hansen

Design Contributors: Laura Mitchell, Dorothy Toth

Publisher's Cataloging in Publication Data

Names: Hansen, Grace, author.

Title: Military attack aircraft / by Grace Hansen.

Description: Minneapolis, Minnesota : Abdo Kids, 2017 | Series: Military aircraft
    & vehicles | Includes bibliographical references and index.

Identifiers: LCCN 2016944099 | ISBN 9781680809336 (lib. bdg.) |
    ISBN 9781680796438 (ebook) | ISBN 9781680797107 (Read-to-me ebook)

Subjects: LCSH: Bombers--Juvenile literature. | Attack planes--Juvenile literature.
    | Airplanes, Military--Juvenile literature. | Fighter planes--Juvenile literature.

Classification: DDC 623.74--dc23

LC record available at http://lccn.loc.gov/2016944099

Table of Contents

Attack Aircraft

Attack aircraft fly low
and slow. They are designed
for close air support. They
deliver **precise** air strikes.

4

5

A-10 Thunderbolt II

The A-10 Thunderbolt II can fly over a battlefield for hours. It supports troops on the ground. It can easily destroy enemy tanks.

6

The A-10 is built around an anti-tank weapon. The GAU-8 Avenger is a seven barrel autocannon. It fires 3,900 armor-piercing shells per minute.

A-10s must fly very low to spot enemy tanks. This makes them **vulnerable** to attacks. A-10s can fly even when they are greatly damaged.

AH-I Super Cobra

The AH-1 Super Cobra was
the first of its kind. It provides
close air support. Its main job
is to help **marines** who are
under fire.

One M197 three-barrel gun sits under the nose. Attachments can hold eight Hellfire missiles. The copilot seated in the front is the gunner.

AH-64D Apache

The AH-64D Apache is another attack helicopter. It is fully loaded and easy to maneuver. It can take on many missions.

The Apache holds two crewmembers. One is the pilot and the other is a gunner. The pilot sits behind the gunner.

The Apache is able to carry 16 Hellfire missiles. One missile can destroy a tank. The chain gun can be controlled by the pilot's helmet display. It aims wherever the pilot is looking.

AH-64D Apache Up Close

- Main four-blade rotor and tail rotor

- A dome holds the Longbow Fire Control Radar system, which gathers and processes battlefield information

- Airspeed: 173 miles per hour (278 km/h)

- Range: 300 miles (483 km)

- Two T700-GE-701 turboshaft engines

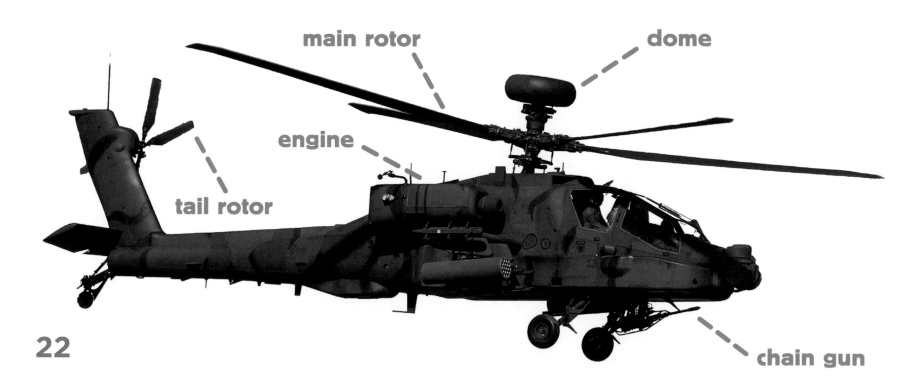

main rotor

dome

engine

tail rotor

chain gun

Glossary

marine – a member of the US Marine Corps.

precise – exact in measuring.

vulnerable – capable of being wounded by a weapon.

23

Index

abdokids.com

Use this code to log on to abdokids.com and access crafts, games, videos, and more!

Abdo Kids Code:
MMK9336